HINDU GODS
AND
GODDESSES

© Rupa Classic India Series 1993
First published 1993 by Rupa & Co.
7/16 Ansari Road, Daryaganj, New Delhi-110 002
Second impression 1998
Set in 9.6 on 12 Palatino by Fototype, Green Park, New Delhi
Printed in India by R.N. Polyplast Pvt. Ltd., Noida

ISBN 81-7167-255-8

Design: KD Prashad
Text and photo research: Ashish Khokar
General Editor: Amrita Kumar

HINDU GODS AND GODDESSES

Rupa & Co

INTRODUCTION

What began, in India, as a celebration of natural elements such as air, water and fire was converted into the worship of cosmic elements such as the sun, moon and stars. The three important gods of the Vedic times were Agni, god of fire; Vayu, god of air and Surya, god of energy or life. These were all sons of Aditi, Mother Nature or earth, wedded to space, Father of Matter or Dyaus. In addition, the nine planets, or Navagraha, were worshipped.

In the post-Vedic phase the concept of the Trimurti emerged. Brahma the Creator, Vishnu the Preserver and Shiva or Mahesh the Destroyer came to denote the three characteristics of God—Generator, Operator, Destructor, or GOD. From these, along with their consorts Saraswati, Lakshmi and Parvati, arose the vast Hindu pantheon. This can be bewildering due to the multiplicity of a single form. For instance, female energy is represented as Parvati, Shakti, Durga, Kali and Meenakshi, and the Tantric cult can be connected to the worship of the union of female energy with male forces.

One of the principal differences between Hinduism and other religions is that Hindu gods and goddesses are not exclusive of one another. Several gods can be worshipped at the same time, as they are all ultimately One.

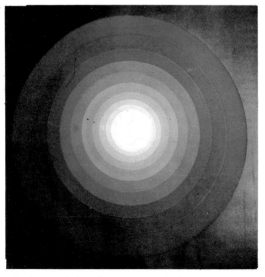

Aum *is the symbol and essence of Hinduism. It means
oneness with the Supreme, the merging of the physical being
with the spiritual.*

The lingam *or phallus of Shiva represents male energy which when combined with the female principle, leads to the creation of mankind. The colour red is auspicious, hence the worship of the Shivalingam with* sindoor.

The colour orange symbolizes renunciation and sainthood and is a predominant colour in Hinduism. The symbology is reflected here in the shilapuja *(stone worship) of a snake god.* Shilapuja *is an integral aspect of Hindu worship and belief.*

A havan, *or holy fire, symbolizes the consumption and purification of most rituals.*

Left: *The pot symbolizes Mother Earth, fertility, abundance; the mango leaves, good fortune. Such symbols are integral to Hindu worship.*

Overleaf: *In the Kulu valley, Himachal Pradesh, the festival coinciding with Dussehra celebrates the triumph of good over evil. Idols are carried from their temples or homes to a ceremonial parade ground.*

Ancestor worship, or honouring and propitiating the memory of the dead, is an integral part of the Hindu tradition. The month of Shraddh, post monsoon, is marked for the observation of this ritual, and temples, like this one in Kutch, are erected in memory of the departed.

BRAHMA THE CREATOR

Brahma was born of the golden egg, Hiranyagarbha. When the egg divided into two parts, heaven and earth were formed. Between these was the sky. He is also said to have sprung from Vishnu's navel, on a lotus, symbolizing rebirth from seeds of past manifeslutions. A Day of Brahma, or Kalpa, is equivalent to 4320 million years.

Brahma is personified by four heads (for four directions) and four arms. He carries a sceptre or bow and like all gods, has a vehicle, the swan. His perch is on Mount Meru and is called Brahmapura or Brahmaloka—the place of Brahma.

He is the lord of scholarship and the four Vedas came from his mouth. His consort is Saraswati, the goddess of higher learning and the arts. Both are thus connected with the art of sculpture, architecture, painting, writing, drama, dance and music, and are worshipped by those seeking spiritual and intellectual advancement.

From Brahma's body came the four castes of the Hindus: The Brahmans or priests from his mouth; the Kshatriyas or soldiers from his arms; the Vaishyas or traders from his thigh and the Sudras or menial workers from his feet.

Today the most important temple of Brahma stands in Pushkar, Rajasthan.

Brahma, the creator of the universe rests on the lotus arising out of Vishnu's navel. At Vishnu's feet is his consort Lakshmi and at his head Saraswati, Brahma's companion. Brahma is the founder of the four Vedas, four castes and four directions.

Saraswati is the goddess of the arts and higher learning. Her vehicle, like Brahma's, is the swan. The veena symbolizes her artistic aspect.

With discus in one hand to root out evil and a mace to wield authority, Vishnu looks after the well-being of all creation.

VISHNU THE PRESERVER

Vishnu is black-blue in body, with four hands — one holding a club, another a conch shell, the third a discus and the fourth a lotus. He rests on the coiled serpent king, Sheshanaga. He covers the universe in three strides: on earth as fire, in the atmosphere as lightning and in the sky us the sun.

He is in control of all universal phenomena and has undisputed power over others. His vehicle is Garuda and his consort, Lakshmi, the goddess of wealth and well-being. Together Vishnu and Lakshmi are a popular duo, worshipped particularly by families seeking material welfare.

Vishnu is the ultimate arbitrator of disputes, between not only human beings but celestial beings too. Thus to his court in the bed of the ocean, come Indra or Narada, with stories and complaints. He intercedes on behalf of others and is the peacemaker. Extremely gentle of nature and personality, he symbolizes tolerance and patience.

He has taken various forms, or avataras, *from time to time, the most popular of which are Rama and Krishna.*

The chief temples of Vishnu worship are Tirupati Venkateshwara in Andhra, Padmanabhan in Kerala and Dwarakadheesh in Gujarat. Krishna and Rama temples are virtually countless.

Lakshmi, consort of Vishnu, symbolizes good fortune and wealth and is the favourite of merchants and traders. On Dewali night, doors of homes are left open in the hope of a chance visit by her.

Right: *Venkateshwara at Tirupati, Andhra Pradesh, is another form of Vishnu.*

18

The ten incarnations of Vishnu: As Matsya the fish, saviour of srishti or creation. Through this form, Vishnu saved the four Vedas from destruction by flood.

As Kurma the tortoise, Vishnu helped the Devas, or pious celestial beings against the Asuras, or devils, when they tried to churn the mythical ocean for nectar that guaranteed eternal life.

As Varaha the boar, Vishnu saved the earth by lifting it on his tusks from the bottom of the ocean where it lay submerged during the fight between the Devas and the Asuras.

Right: *As Narasimha, half lion, half man, Vishnu saved his devotee Prahlad from his evil father Hiranyakashyapu.*

As Vamana the dwarf, Vishnu asked King Bali for a mere three steps of the earth. When he assumed his real form, he covered the whole earth in one step, thus humbling the king.

Right: As Parashurama, or Rama with the axe, Vishnu annihilated the demons in their battle with the gods. Another account holds that he took this form to rid the world of oppression by kings.

As Rama, he led the victory of good over evil. The epic
Ramayana *is based on this seventh incarnation of Vishnu.*

As Krishna, he became the hero of the battle between the warring brothers, the Pandavas and the Kauravas, as related in the epic, the Mahabarata.

As Gautama Buddha, the Enlightened One, he showed the path of righteousness and set the course for a new religion, Buddhism.

Kalki, the tenth incarnation of Vishnu is yet to manifest itself. It is believed that it will be in the form of a horseman who will appear when the world is near its end and save it from extinction.

Krishna's flute symbolizes the soul. His dallying with the gopis (milkmaids) of Vrindavan gave him the image of the eternal lover.

Right: *Krishna floating on a betel leaf is symbolic of his transfer across the Yamuna river to Gokul by Vasudeva.*

Krishna with sister Subhadra and brother Balarama are worshipped as a trio at the Jagannath temple, Puri, Orissa.

Left: *At Dwarka, Krishna is worshipped as Dwarkadheesh Thakur. This aspect of Krishna worship is marked by austerity and devotion.*

Krishna as Sarthi (charioteer) to Arjuna in the great battle at Kurukshetra. It was during this battle that he delivered a sermon to Arjuna that is immortalized in the Bhagavad Gita.

Right: *Hanuman, the monkey-god is known for his devotion to Rama. He is the epitome of selfless dedication.*

SHIVA THE DESTROYER

It is Shiva's power of destruction that regenerates. He is Mahayogi or patron saint of all yogis. He is represented by the lingam which denotes male energy and reproduction. His consort is Parvati, Shakti or female energy. The fusion of the two leads to life. Hence Shiva is propitiated for productivity and growth of the human race.

Mount Kailasha, in the upper reaches of the Himalayas is his abode. His vehicle is the white bull and he is the lord of all animals. Thus in his entourage are lions, snakes and bears. He is called Nilakantha, or the blue-throated one because in the churning of the ocean he drank the poison which would otherwise have destroyed the universe. Shiva's anger is legendary. He is also the Digambara, the naked-ascetic. The holy river Ganga sprouts from his matted locks. The moon and stars adorn his crown. As Nataraja, he is the lord of dance.

His two sons are Kartikeya, or Murugan, and Ganesha. Ganesha is the remover of all obstacles and Kartikeya is the brave warrior, the lord of war.

From Amarnath to Chidambaram, from Thanjavur to Kashmir, his temples abound. His consort Parvati is no less important and is celebrated from Jammu-Vaishnodevi as Durga to Madurai, as Meenakshi.

Shiva and Parvati represent the union of male and female energies, the production and growth of the human race. Their abode is in the Himalayas.

Shilapuja *of the* Shivalingam *as represented at a cave in Aurangabad, Maharashtra.*

Left: *The concept of cosmic forces merging with divine elements is depicted here with the sun, moon and stars and the auspicious swastika under the gaze of Shiva.*

Kartikeya, elder son of Shiva and Parvati is annihilator of evil. The spear denotes his warrior-like qualities; the peacock is his vehicle. In south India he is referred to as Murugan.

Right: *Parvati, consort of Shiva, is the all-encompassing female energy, worshipped as Mother Nature. She is the eternal bride in red.*

The Gangaur festival of Rajasthan celebrates Gauri, the unwed form of Parvati. For young girls seeking husbands, this is an important occasion.

Right: *Parvati as Mariamma, the goddess of poxes, who grants freedom from sickness.*

In south India, Parvati becomes Meenakshi, the one with the parrot, symbolizing prosperity and fertility.

Right: *For nomads she takes the form of Trimbakeshwari, seen here at a temple in Nasik, Maharashtra.*

One of the forms of Parvati (Shakti) is Durga astride a tiger, destroyer of evil and protector of the faithful. In this form she is also called Shairon wali Mata.

Left: *In West Bengal she is Kali, the fierce form of female energy.*

Overleaf: *During Durga Puja, the goddess is immersed in the holy waters and thus returned to nature.*

Half man, half elephant, Ganesha is the younger son of Shiva and Parvati. He adores food and his vehicle is the rat. He is the god of wisdom and the remover of obstacles. In western India he is worshipped as Ganapati.

Shiva as Bhairav, the tantric-ascetic, worshipped in primitive form in a cave in Jodhpur, Rajasthan.

Left: *Purification, in Hinduism, is through fire or water. Thus the cities along the holy river Ganga are pilgrim centres. In Benares, the city of Shaivism, the ghats are a core area for acts of ablution.*

*Snake worship is prevalent in east and south India.
Nagapanchami is an important festival dedicated to snake
gods and goddesses.*

Raudra Shiva is Shiva in anger, the howler. The worship of Raudra Shiva is marked by self-sacrifices, austerities and penance.

Ravana, the ten-headed king of Lanka was a devotee of Shiva. He is worshipped in this aspect in south India.

Left: *Shiva delivers devotee Markandeya from evil, striking a pose similar to his persona as the lord of dance, Nataraja. Shiva is also protector of the animal kingdom.*

Saints and sages are integral to the Hindu tradition.
Shankaracharya inspired the formation of a sect that stresses
on the finer points of Hindu philosophy.

Vishwakarma is worshipped by those involved in mechanical labour.

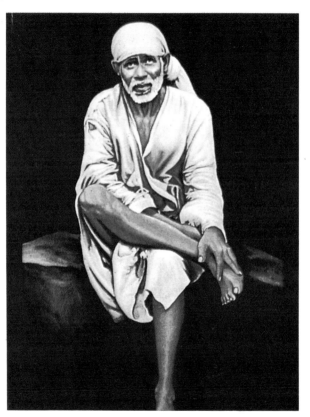

Saibaba preached communal harmony and togetherness.

THE HINDU PANTHEON

THE COSMIC TRINITY

Surya, god of energy
Agni, god of fire
Vayu, god of air

THE HINDU TRINITY

The Creator, his manifestations and his family

Brahma, creator of the universe
Saraswati, his consort, goddess of learning
Swan, Saraswati's vehicle

The Preserver, his manifestations and his family

Vishnu, preserver of the universe
Lakshmi, his consort, goddess of wealth

Matsya the fish, first incarnation of Vishnu
Kurma the tortoise, second incarnation of Vishnu
Varaha the boar, third incarnation of Vishnu
Narasimha, half lion, half man, fourth incarnation of Vishnu
Vamana the dwarf, fifth incarnation of Vishnu

Parashurama, the slayer, sixth incarnation of Vishnu
Rama, the king who vanquished Ravana, seventh incarnation
of Vishnu
Krishna, the cowherd warrior, eighth incarnation of Vishnu
Buddha, the Enlightened, ninth incarnation of Vishnu
Kalki, the last (yet to come) incarnation of Vishnu

Balarama, brother of Krishna
Lakshmana, brother of Rama
Ravana, the ten-headed king of Lanka
Radha, devotee-lover of Krishna
Rukmini, wife of Krishna
Sita, daughter of Janak, and wife of Rama

Hanuman, the monkey-god of the Ramayana
Jatayu, saviour of Sita
Garuda, vehicle of Vishnu and Lakshmi
Sheshanaga, the serpent-king on whom Vishnu rests

The Destroyer, his manifestations and his family

Shiva, destroyer of the universe
Mahesh, another name for Shiva
Bhairav, the ascetic form of Shiva
Raudradeva, the angry form of Shiva
Nataraja, Shiva as the lord of dance

Parvati, Shiva's consort and Shakti (female energy)
Durga, a form of Shakti, astride a lion
Kali, destroyer of evil, another form of Shakti
Meenakshi, at Madurai, a representation of Shakti or Parvati
Uma, daughter of the mountains, wife of Shiva (Parvati)
Ganesha, elephant-headed son of Shiva and Parvati,
                              remover of obstacles
Kartikeya, son of Shiva and Parvati, warrior-annihilator
Nandi, the bull, Shiva's vehicle

NAVAGRAHA OR THE NINE PLANETS

Surya, the sun
Soma, the moon
Buddha, Mercury
Sukra, Venus
Mangala, Mars
Brahspati, Jupiter
Shani, Saturn
Rahu, dragon's head
Ketu, dragon's tail